Life Cycles

A Salmon's Life Cycle

by Jamie Rice

C000261646

Bullfrog Books

Ideas for Parents and Teachers

Bullfrog Books let children practice reading informational text at the earliest reading levels. Repetition, familiar words, and photo labels support early readers.

Before Reading
- Discuss the cover photo. What does it tell them?
- Look at the picture glossary together. Read and discuss the words.

Read the Book
- "Walk" through the book and look at the photos. Let the child ask questions. Point out the photo labels.
- Read the book to the child, or have him or her read independently.

After Reading
- Prompt the child to think more. Ask: Salmon have seven life stages. Can you name them?

Bullfrog Books are published by Jump!
5357 Penn Avenue South
Minneapolis, MN 55419
www.jumplibrary.com

Copyright © 2023 Jump! International copyright reserved in all countries. No part of this book may be reproduced in any form without written permission from the publisher.

Library of Congress Cataloging-in-Publication Data

Names: Rice, Jamie, author.
Title: A salmon's life cycle / Jamie Rice.
Description: Bullfrog books.
Minneapolis, MN: Jump!, Inc., [2023]
Series: Life cycles | Includes index.
Audience: Ages 5–8
Identifiers: LCCN 2021048384 (print)
LCCN 2021048385 (ebook)
ISBN 9781636908373 (hardcover)
ISBN 9781636908380 (paperback)
ISBN 9781636908397 (ebook)
Subjects: LCSH: Salmon—Life cycles
Juvenile literature.
Classification: LCC QL638.S2 R495 2023 (print)
LCC QL638.S2 (ebook)
DDC 597.5/5156—dc23/eng/20211001
LC record available at
https://lccn.loc.gov/2021048384
LC ebook record available at
https://lccn.loc.gov/2021048385

Editor: Eliza Leahy
Designer: Emma Bersie

Photo Credits: Design Pics Inc/Alamy, cover, 4, 15, 16–17, 19, 22, 23bl; Sergey Uryadnikov/Shutterstock, 1; Zykov _ Vladimir/Shutterstock, 3 (top), 20–21, 23tl; Ippeito/Dreamstime, 3 (bottom); Fernando Lessa/Alamy, 5, 8–9, 22, 23tr; yamaoyaji/Shutterstock, 6–7, 22; jack perks/Alamy, 10–11, 22; Minden Pictures/SuperStock, 12–13, 22; Daisuke Kurashima/Dreamstime, 14, 22; Marcos Franchetti/Dreamstime, 18, 23br; Kevin Wells Photography/Shutterstock, 24.

Printed in the United States of America at Corporate Graphics in North Mankato, Minnesota.

Table of Contents

From Stream to Sea

This fish is a salmon.

It swims in a stream.

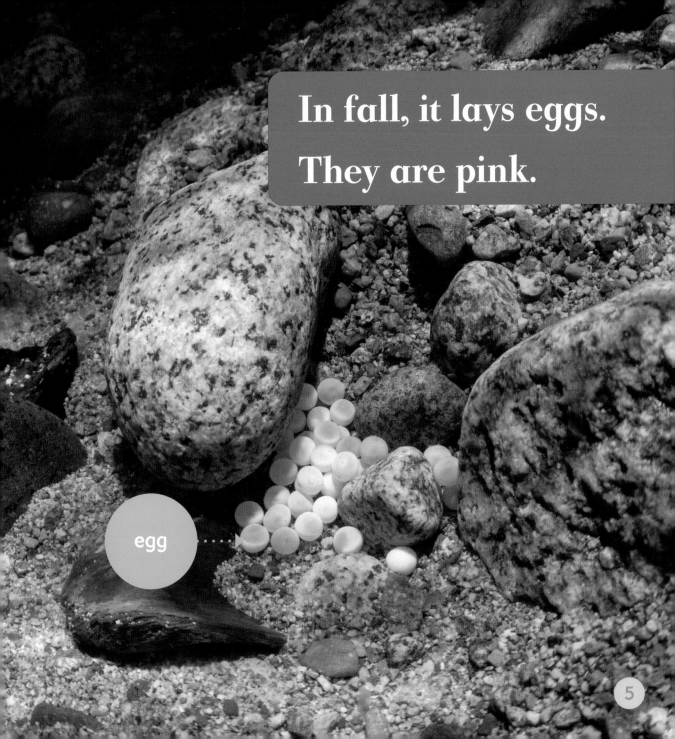

In fall, it lays eggs.
They are pink.

egg

5

alevin

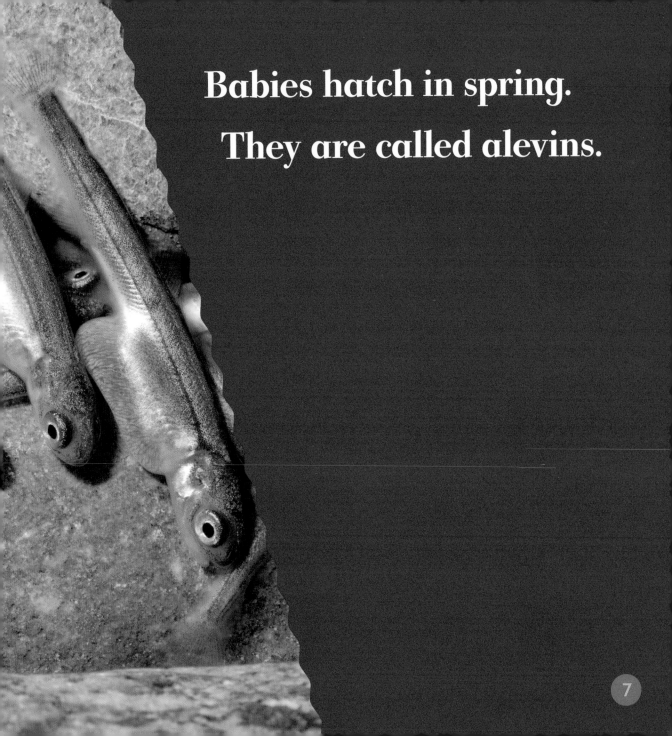

Babies hatch in spring.
They are called alevins.

They eat bugs and plants.

They grow.

Now they are fry!

fry

parr

They grow bigger.
We call them parr.

A year goes by.
Now they are smolts.
They swim to the ocean.

smolts

13

They live in the ocean.

They grow into adults.

They swim in schools.

school

Years go by.
Now they are
spawning adults.
This one turns red.

It swims upstream.

It goes to the stream it was born in.

It digs with its tail.

It makes a nest.

nest

It lays eggs.
The life cycle starts again!

Life Cycle of a Salmon

A salmon's life cycle has seven stages. Take a look!

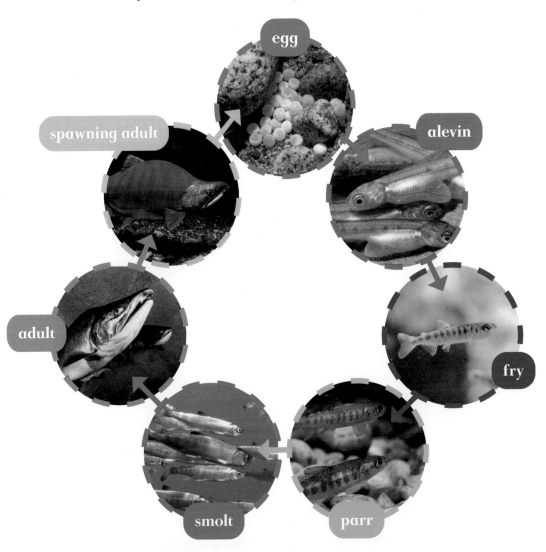

Picture Glossary

hatch
To break out of eggs.

life cycle
The series of changes each living thing goes through from birth to death.

spawning adults
Adults that are able to produce young.

upstream
Against the current and toward the source of a stream or river.

Index

To Learn More

Finding more information is as easy as 1, 2, 3.

❶ Go to www.factsurfer.com

❷ Enter "asalmon'slifecycle" into the search box.

❸ Choose your book to see a list of websites.